CULTURE IS BEAUTIFUL

Look Beyond the Surface

Audith C Johnson

COPYRIGHTS & CREDITS

CULTURE IS BEAUTIFUL: Look Beyond the Surface

Copyright © 2025. Audith C Johnson. All rights reserved

No part of this book may be used or reproduced by any means, graphic, electronic, or mechanical, including photocopying, recording, taping, or by any information storage retrieval system without the written permission of the author except in the case of brief quotations embodied in critical articles and reviews.

For information contact:

<u>Audith C Johnson</u>
Email: audiejohns12@comcast.net
Cover Design: Sylvia M Dallas - The Publisher's Notebook Limited
Book Formatting: Sylvia M Dallas - The Publisher's Notebook Limited
Editing: Minette Lawrence

ISBN: 979-8-218-65228-9(paperback)
979-8-218-65229-6(ebook)

Image Sources; Cover Image & Chapter 1 -
AI generated collage (DALL-E)
Chapters 2-11 - pixabay.com

DEDICATION

I dedicate this book to the young people I have met, taught, and mentored and to those who will read it.

…to the young at heart and any person who will want to gain insight by looking at culture and how it can affect us all….

Audith C. Johnson

TABLE OF CONTENTS

ACKNOWLEDGMENTS	I
INTRODUCTION	Ii
1. Same But Different	1
2. Hey, Is Culture A Legal Thing?	9
3. Values Here, Values There…	13
4. Is It Religiosity Or Spirituality? - What's The Difference?	17
5. What Has Emotion Got To Do With It?	21
6. Finances, Is It Relevant To Our Health?	25
7. What Does History And Bibliology Have To Do With Us Now?	29
8. Eating: I Like That; No! No, I Love That	37
9. Language / Communication - Do We Understand Each Other?	41
10. Glossary	55
11. Bibliography	68
12. About The Author	71

ACKNOWLEDGMENTS

Special thanks to my spiritual parents, Apostle Dr. Alph and Bishop Celeste Lukau, for their encouragement in remaining tenacious in what I started.

In addition, I am grateful to my local church leaders, Pastor Ericka Sanders and Minister Glorious (Michelle Campbell), for their constant motivation.

I want to thank Pastor Minett Lawrence (author, lawyer, businesswoman, and editor) for her legal advice and the points she provided as she edited the book.

I am grateful to my family for always seeing the best in me. I also want to thank my friend, Janet Smith-Bray, who consistently encouraged and understood my goals.

I especially appreciate all my teachers' colleagues and those with whom I served in our communities and church. These collaborative efforts have opened and strengthened my vision for this book.

Lastly, I am grateful to my daughter for cheering me on and being proud of all my involvement, which made me stronger and a better leader.

Grateful

Audith C. Johnson

INTRODUCTION

Truly, it is not easy writing about culture. However, I want to establish that Culture is Beautiful if we were to review it from the beginning of time to the present. The more I consider the topic, the more I realize that we are all different yet vastly similar.

I aim to display that while we are different, we are similar and can cohabit and enhance each other regardless of the daily circumstances.

It can present intrigue. Once viewed closely, we can realize that all the factors we describe in the book can result in an insatiable desire to learn about others and their way of life.

Consequently, we will learn that we use different terms, which can mean the same things in given situations. Some situations are viewed similarly, yet our ways of operations can differ. For example, our emotions, finances, eating, language, and many natural ways of life may produce different results. It is simply how we communicate our actions.

In addition, local and regional laws may play an integral part in our daily operations. That is, the laws of a particular land can induce a person, company, or family's behavior.

As we continue through the book, we will view that our values also aid in decision-making for our families, job choices, friends, and many other aspects of our daily lives.

Of course, religion or spirituality influences our consistent reactions and views. I will aim to outline that concept in that chapter.

What adds to our intrigue is the words we use to express ourselves, especially when considering the trigonometry of writing and speaking these words. The grammar and style of writing that typify different languages are quite insightful and will raise one's interest in learning more. For example, some Asian cultures write from right to left, while in Western culture, we continue to pen our information from left to right.

Interestingly, we can all gather in one place and realize that we understand each other, even though there may be differences. If we were to travel back in time, especially to Biblical times: Acts Chapter 2 to be specific – we would notice people of all cultures were in that one setting. Different languages were spoken and yet they were of one accord.

Spiritually, we view things daily from our own experiences. We are different physically, yet we are all spiritual beings. The Bible expounds on this in many of its stories. People were always seeking higher power. I find Dr. Alph Lukau's, (a spiritual and renowned Bible scholar) teaching on spirituality very intriguing; he explains how much we are spiritual beings and biblically dissects the concept for great understanding. The Book of Hebrews 11 verse 3 states, "Through faith, we understand that the worlds were framed by the word of God so that things which are seen were not made of things which do appear". This scripture can be a start at looking through Dr. Lukau's lens.

It is food for thought and can pique your interest in knowing that humans are spiritual beings. Globally, we can realize that there are many different religious concepts or groups as man continues to find himself spiritually.

Now, I hope you will gain from my world of research and teaching. It is a pleasure to aim to ignite other interests among nations or cultures.

Another aim is:

- to motivate cross-cultural exchanges

- to promote a greater understanding of each other's surroundings; and

- to develop a healthy curiosity for the things that affect diverse yet similar people.

SELF-REFLECTION QUESTIONS

1. Have you ever viewed culture differently?
   _____

2. What is culture to you?
   _____
   _____

3. Do you enjoy working in a diverse setting?
   _____
   _____

4. Are you ready to explore the possibilities as you read this book?
   _____
   _____

SAME BUT DIFFERENT

We are the same. We come from the same source: God. God is our Father. We may choose to interpret this ideology differently, but everyone looks to a divine source. We will examine this in a later chapter.

Should we rationalize it in the natural sense, we begin life in a woman's womb. A womb carries the child until birth. However, the environment starts to influence and shape the child upon birth.

SAME. SOURCE. THE. WOMB. BUT. SHAPED. BY. OUR. SURROUNDINGS.

From the beginning, man has sought to communicate with a divine being in his bid for survival. Many scientific and behavioral management theorists have articulated the means for survival and connection. Abraham Maslow, an American Psychologist, developed the Hierarchy of Needs Pyramid. Though this theory is aimed primarily at gauging workplace behavior, the principle applies equally to making choices in our daily lives.

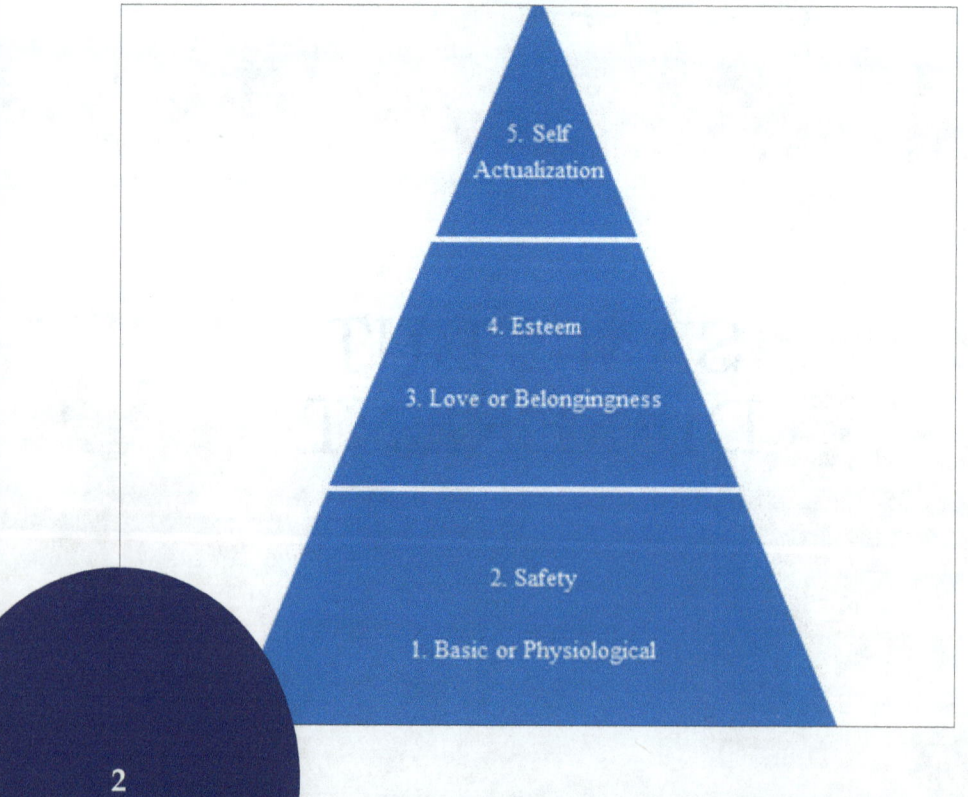

In Maslow's Hierarchy, Basic or Physiological Needs are deemed the first on the ladder of success. That was defined as the need to satisfy hunger and thirst. Satisfying these areas of need is essential for daily survival. However, let us think beyond that.

Satisfying hunger and thirst can be viewed as meeting the need for anything desired. We naturally want to satisfy our hunger for success, hunger for connection, or hunger for survival. Though the other parts of the hierarchy speak to hunger or needs at different levels, I want to focus first on this basic level. Without the first level, there is no survival.

Notably, Maslow meant well in saying that it was for hunger and thirst. Physical hunger or thirst may have been the primary focus for the basic needs; however, it can be wise to think beyond those two components. At any given time, a person can hunger for emotional health, financial well-being, spiritual connection or strength, educational stability, and other similar attributes.

So, we are the same. We hunger for something. We thirst for something. Yet we are so different in the way we operate. One can allude to the innate self or how man was socialized from ages 0-5. Studies show that a child's development takes place during these years. For example, an adult's life can attract consistent catastrophes if they are not exposed to a healthy environment. Of course, each child's development will vary based on their exposure to diverse environments.

As we can see and agree, though we are humans, our thought processes may not look alike. Why? We ask. Thoughts are formed from what we see, hear, and share in our formative years. Consequently, we develop as we learn from formal and informal environments.

Though we form our thoughts from early learning, these can be reshaped. We can now revisit Maslow's Hierarchy or his Motivation Theory. On this hierarchy, Maslow shares that as we gain satisfaction at each level, we can move to the next. However, since we may differ in our needs, we may display an inability to move up the pyramid, especially if unresolved issues are in our path. Many people are extremely hurt, making it difficult to step forward. If we are not similarly challenged, we can seek ways or resources to help the person in need.

Further studies on Maslow's Hierarchy highlight that when one becomes self-actualized, life changes do not guarantee a reversal of each level of success. For instance, a person's status may change in the event of bankruptcy, the death of a loved one, job loss, adopting a different culture once one has migrated to a different country, or other personal lifestyle changes.

Bankruptcy is sometimes inevitable in a person's life. When this occurs, a person may revert to the basic needs or descend to another level of the ladder.

Death is also inevitable. Sometimes death happens unexpectedly. A person may not have been properly prepared for the death of a loved one. Life insurance, Will, and other financially sensitive testamentary documents may not have been established so surviving family members can effectively carry on their daily lives.

Job loss is another frequent uncontrollable issue; an employer may have no choice but to downsize or reorganize his business due to varying market setbacks. Likewise, some employers may furlough their workers. Furlough is a temporary interruption where the worker may be called back to work.

To ease the furloughed worker's immediate financial stress, the company may provide at least two weeks of salary and have the worker choose to work elsewhere while he awaits a callback. Of course, there is no guarantee that the worker will gain employment during this waiting period, or if he or she will be called back to work. During the COVID-19 pandemic, many organizations such as hotels, airlines, retailers, and similar businesses furloughed their workers, as it was the best choice given the sudden and unexpected changes in the global economy.

Adopting a different culture or migrating to a new country can pose similar setbacks for an individual due to differences in laws, job-eligibility requirements, language barriers, and suitable and available gainful jobs, among other impediments.

During these times, a sense of community is needed. Most countries require similar documentation to obtain the jobs that candidates need. Family members and friends may help; however, it will be wise for an applicant to focus on gaining employment for his sustenance. Here, we can incorporate Maslow's aim through the Hierarchical chart.

The second level on the ladder is safety. Therefore, having a job provides financial safety and security. Receiving a paycheck bi-weekly, weekly, monthly, and bi-monthly can develop confidence in maintaining oneself or the family.

From safety to love or belonging; to esteem, and self-actualization.

Often, the achievement level switches on the hierarchy. For example, a person may hold himself in high esteem and value what he does; but have no regard for love or belonging. This predilection can be due to a person's value system or be purely environmental.

It is vital to note that many churches and non-profit organizations are set up to help individuals meet their needs. To develop our communities, we can help someone find these resources. If we do not have direct knowledge about the correct organizations for the problem; we can seek it out, and "…we shall find it".

Organizations have structured help for individuals in need. We live in an era where everyone is considered important, and we are indeed important. The North American school system's inclusion model states that "no one is left behind". Importantly, while no one is forgotten, everyone's need levels may differ.

Are we among the subset willing to help someone who needs help? Or are we willing to step in, even though we may not have the resources to help? No man is an island; an adage that still rings true in my ear. It is also a popular song by Joan Baez. We need each other. We do not have to be the same. Your strength helps somebody's weakness. Your abundance is the answer to a friend's lack. Knowledge and resources can help another person's individual needs. Are you getting the picture?

In Joan Baez's song, "No Man Is an Island", a quote from the lyrics is helpful:

> "No man is an island entire of itself
> Every man is a piece of the continent
> A part of the main"

Thought-provoking, correct?

We are the same yet different as we make up this world of huge cultural differences. We differ due to our environment, experiences, and education. By association, we can change or advance. Again, we need each other.

A family of seven children with the same parents can have different viewpoints. Likewise, employees trained in the same way in one class can provide different outputs. An organization may have one goal; however, each department has a distinct role in seeing it come to fruition.

While the seven children can display vast differences in their personalities, their thinking processes may be similar, but each may operate differently due to his studies, environment, and contacts.

Yes, our differences make the world an interesting place to live. We can use these differences to empower each other. We are the same. We are similar. Our approach to achieving results may differ due to our association, early socialization, actualization, and spirituality. It is like the body. The knee cannot operate without the upper leg and calves. The head cannot effectively function without the neck.

While everyone may have his customs or practices, communities must endeavor to understand each other. The norm in one community may not be the same for its neighbors. For example, Western or Caribbean culture has practiced shaking hands in formal settings as a greeting or a sign of acknowledgment. In contrast, some Eastern cultures may bow in greeting or as acknowledgment—some hug, while others are offended by that practice.

As we learn to understand each other, we will become more tolerant of our neighbors' behavior

> A neighbor is anyone with whom we communicate daily.

SELF REFLECTION QUESTIONS

1. What makes you different from those around you?

   _____

   _____

   _____

2. Do you have a circle of friends with the same likes?

   _____

   _____

   _____

3. At what stage are you on Maslow's Hierarchy?

   _____

4. Do you see yourself achieving the next step soon or in the next five years?

_____
_____
_____

2

HEY, IS CULTURE A LEGAL THING?

Culture is our various ways of life. What is the culture of your home? What is the culture of your community? What is the culture within your country, island, or continent? No matter how we view it; we all have some form of legal structure that guides the path. This is a written or unwritten expectation in our environment.

The words of the adage; "when in Rome, do as the Romans do" challenge us to meet and satisfy hidden expectations. Though it is not a direct legal issue, it is an acceptable way of life. For example, living in the United States compels a behavior that encourages immigrants to learn the language in the American way to be relevant or beneficial in community or work settings. Please note I will discuss language in depth in a later chapter.

We can refer to a specific example of Caribbean or European immigrants. This population is taught the English Language, the British way. It is classified as "the Queen's English." Therefore, though this community speaks English, the language is different. Some spellings are different, and synonyms can be different, among other language insights.

The word 'lodge' can mean a lodging or place to stay/accommodation/cabin. The lodge is also a meeting place for organizations such as the Freemasons. However, it can be used in the verb form in the Caribbean and British cultures. One example is, "I lodged my cash today at Nova Scotia Bank", while the American culture may say, "I deposited my cash at so and so bank". So, lodging and depositing are synonymous across cultures when used in the verb tense. It can be seen as a norm versus another. It is the hidden legality within each culture.

Notably, the American system's use of the verb tense for lodge in court appeals, for example: "...I lodged an appeal...", while the Canadians, say, "I filed an appeal". So, the use is not incorrect. It is only used differently in each culture.

Is the above considered legal? It is not necessarily the way of life in that given space. We will discuss the matter of language in a later chapter. In the study of Law, there are rules of interpretation that accommodate cultural differences in discerning the meaning of a word. Cultural context and personal influences are considered when arriving at the meaning or purpose of the words used in a legal document.

Legality can be considered the norm in a society, and some not. Some norms are considered taboo. Some tabooed traditional practices among cultures are classified as witchcraft. It is called different names across cultures. The Haitians call it Voodoo, and the Jamaicans, Obeah. While the activity is sometimes taboo, it can be expected. As it is considered a norm, it is never a practice that can be enforced or challenged in court. It is a spiritual thing. Battles are won or lost in the spiritual realm.

Arguably, spirituality is the norm in different cultures; however, some spiritual practices such as Christianity are taboo in some cultures, especially Eastern communities. Some Christians practice underground worship instead of openly declaring their beliefs. So far, the American system considers Christianity and other forms of worship openly as it is said to be a free country. Other developed countries and societies continue to review laws.

Legal systems are designed to defend victims, or the less fortunate. It is also to maintain order. An example of an order being maintained is a driver required to obtain a driver's license or national identification card. Hence, a country's order is maintained since each card has an expiration date. A citizen is expected to renew his card before or on the expiration date to be relevant in that society or show he belongs to that nation, population, or culture. It aids in keeping count of a given population, so the governmental bodies can design structural systems to serve that community or country. The legal system does create order.

Another legal form in each society is the tariffs and fees paid across cultures as travelers enjoy other nations. We will look at this briefly in another chapter.

So, I posit that culture, or our way of life, is legal.

SELF REFLECTION QUESTIONS

1. Do you view culture as legal?
   _____

2. What is your view?
   _____
   _____

3. Can you find references to validate your thought process?
   _____

   _____

   _____

VALUES HERE, VALUES THERE...

Previously, we saw values could be shaped by early socialization, cultural norms, spiritual society, educational institutions, and our environment; it is safe to view whether they can become ingrained or otherwise. We all have choices. We can choose right from wrong. We can seek peace, love, joy, or what is right.

Values within a family unit can be the same yet divided or different. A child or children can be taught certain values during their youth; however, they may choose to seek their path as adults. Sometimes, a family disowns a member because they no longer want to be identified with that person's newfound way of life, or the other does not want to be identified with their past, such as a poor background.

Value systems can be formed among firstborn, second-born, third-born, and last-born.

Although each child's growth stage has different milestones and skills – their personality traits may differ based on where they fall in the family. For example, studies show that the first child often displays dominant and commanding traits. The second or middle child seeks peace or goes with the flow. The last child is considered spoiled or favored to do his own thing. He also appears to be happier than the others due to the laissez-faire governance given to him. Consequently, these factors can lead to each child developing differently.

Values are also seen when some countries allow their citizens to travel easily to another country without a visa or any form of prior authorization for legal entry. Another country may not allow citizens to travel due to the type of governmental system in place. Whether it is a capitalist, communist, socialist, monarchist, or democratic make-up, political systems shape each population's values. Notably, some countries such as America have choices while others do not due to the country's governance.

In some countries, the style of dress is important. In others, it is not so important once the individual is comfortable with him or herself.

For instance, the British are notoriously known to wear hats, especially for formal occasions, while Americans have a choice. Some churches or religious sects expect their members to wear headwear. We can see this in more rigid evangelical churches where women must wear hats and long dresses.

Catholic Bishops wear skull caps or zucchetto to keep their heads warm since they practice shaving their heads.

Muslim worshippers and their guests cover their heads to enter a place of worship.

Jews wear a skull cap to worship and show reverence to God: a symbol of their Jewish identity, and humility. Anglican women wear a chapel veil or mantilla to show submission.

Each headpiece has its meaning.

Each society or group interprets its reasoning for its practices. As a result, values determine what is important. Do we respect each other's values?

Love is key for us to survive in multicultural societies. We must value respecting each other. The same is true when we travel to different nations or countries. Respect and enjoy each other.

SELF REFLECTION QUESTIONS

1. Do you think you have developed a different value system from your family members?

   _____

2. If so, please describe it.

   _____

   _____

   _____

   _____

3. If you have gained more insight, name ways you can use these values to improve life.

_____

_____

_____

4. Can you find an article or name a book or magazine that gives you a broader perspective?

_____

_____

IS IT RELIGIOSITY OR SPIRITUALITY? - WHAT'S THE DIFFERENCE?

There is general agreement that "religion" can be a structure of rules and bylaws for its adherents to govern their way of thinking and serving. At the same time "spirituality" means to be connected to the Divine and being led by God.

Dictionaries and studies say that:

RELIGION	*SPIRITUALITY*
Religion is an organized system of beliefs, practices, and rituals often associated with a particular faith	Spirituality is a more personal and individual experience of the sacred and the divine.
Religion is often about who's in and who's out, creating a worldview steeped in "us against them."	Spirituality rejects this dualism and speaks of us and them…in "oneness"
Religion is often about loyalty to institutions, clergy, and rules	Spirituality is based only on love and not fear. Dotted throughout religion, there is fear …
Religion tells you the truth, spirituality allows you to discover it. As opposed to telling you…	There are no rules to spirituality. As opposed to following a specific ideology or a set of religious rules.

In other words, religion is known to be governed by rules and does not promote free thinking and creativity. In some practices, members are ostracized if they do not follow the rules.

On the other hand, spirituality gives a free way to commune with God and man. Individuals express themselves to God through prayer and meditation. They also impart their experiences to others through testimonies and lifestyles. It is important to note that one section of the study shared that spirituality is a connotation of love and not fear. God is love. Humans can freely communicate with God and receive answers to prayers that bring peace, joy, and happiness. No fear only trust that God answers prayers.

Conversely, each society appreciates one or the other or none. Although we are the same about seeking spirituality, though different, we recognize there is a God. Bible scholar, Dr. Alph Lukau says "We are spiritual beings living in a physical body." (paraphrased). In other words, we existed before we were physically on earth. One understanding is that if one says they had a Déjà vu, it can mean the event occurred before their physical time on Earth. While we live on earth, things happen around us such as dreams and visions, which ultimately manifest later unless we are disobedient to God's Word, we may not enjoy the "fruits of our labor".

Another understanding of us being spiritual beings is that we can tap into God's supernatural realm and pray about things that concern us. We can see in the spiritual world to assist us with guiding, coaching, and teaching those in need. However, there is a catch to that, Dr. Alph says that we need to have a relationship with the Lord through reading, meditating, and praying the Word of God over situations. That is, we can speak things into being as though they were. (Genesis 1:1-31) and Romans 4:17 KJV

Conversely, other religions recognize it; however, many have chosen religious preferences such as using another text instead of the Bible as their guide. For example, Muslims use the Quran as the Holy book of Islam. Islamic culture reveres Jesus, whom they call Isa as a holy prophet, and Mary, Jesus' mother: Mariam as a Holy woman.

The debate still rests around the Holy Bible being the true Word of God.

SELF REFLECTION QUESTIONS

1. What does religion mean to you?

_____

_____

_____

2. What does spirituality mean to you?

_____

_____

_____

3. Do you have other views and why?

_____

_____

_____

_____

4. In what way are you inspired to explore the information shared?

_____

_____

_____

_____

5

WHAT HAS EMOTION GOT TO DO WITH IT?

Emotions. Emotions. Our emotional state is determined by our mindset, values, beliefs, and current state of mind; however, an individual can practice control.

According to the Oxford Dictionary, "Emotion is a natural instinctive state of mind derived from one's circumstances, mood, or relationships with others".

It continued to explain that no conclusive scientific proof of some emotional behaviors has been found. Psycho-physiologist and Behaviorist William James' views have been widely used for the issue. James' analysis concludes that emotional behaviors are due to a subject's location and experiences.

However, we can choose whether to act on our knowledge or our mindset. We can choose to control our thinking or behavior. Another way is to own the emotion and make things right. When we use empathy, our negative emotions can be easily portrayed positively. Some studies show that we gain positive results when phrases such as, "I understand…" are used to resolve a conflict. This statement can set the tone for an empathetic message or control an agreement. Of course, the tone of this expression remains vital to winning trust.

Interestingly, many conflicts can be resolved amicably if responses remain positive. The Bible says, "A soft answer turns away wrath".

Steven Covey says, "Seek first to understand before you can be understood" (paraphrased).

Should understanding be a normal way of life? Understanding others or those with whom we interact, and how they interact is pertinent to maintaining better communication.

We find in a time of migration and immigration across cultures, misunderstandings occur. On one hand, it is the language or language barrier. On the other hand, it is the style of expressing oneself.

In some countries, people slur or draw their speech, while in others they may speak too fast.

Some use a high pitch and others low. Another barrier may be the communicator's accent. Though the language is the same, the receiver of the message may block the message as they are not familiar with the accents or are prejudiced against a certain sound.

So, when communication gaps are realized, emotions can be displayed negatively or positively. Some English-speaking cultures may not appreciate that another speaks their language if the sound differs. They may conclude that the other person is uneducated. Consequently, the misunderstood subject can choose not to respond emotionally. This response can aid in deflating the conflict.

These issues can be discussed at length. However, let us look at the negative emotions, especially if the communicator was not schooled for such an environment; or socially trained to communicate with a specific community or environment.

Previously, many populations were unfairly treated based on their ability. As a former teacher, trainer, coach, and mentor, I have seen grave misunderstandings arise because a leader or teacher may not have been trained to handle a situation with a student or mentee.

For example, an Asperger or autistic student can be hugely misunderstood if the teacher is not trained to identify the issues and resolve them appropriately. Some cultures do not recognize these students or do not have the resources or funds to serve this population, so they get overlooked or ostracized. We are grateful for the American system that has enforced laws for this population. It is with gratitude that many societies or communities have been received when they have stepped in with their resources.

Emotions can enrage both the presenter and receiver. Neither understands the other. In our modern world, it is vital to know the laws and ways of life of others to intelligibly communicate with those in school, at work, or at play.

Another sector of society is the underprivileged or poor. Poor does not necessarily mean a person is without money; it can mean scarcity of other essential goods or services. This population occasionally never appears in public as they may fear being misunderstood. Due to a lack of communication or exposure, a subject's emotional state may display negative behavioral patterns during conflicts.

Ultimately, as the world has grown over the centuries, nations need to seek to understand each other and serve well politically, spiritually, emotionally, educationally, societally, financially, and other necessary allies to create unity or a better world.

SELF REFLECTION QUESTIONS

1. What is emotion to you?

_____

_____

_____

2. Would you like to see more discussion of this topic in the next volume?

_____

3. Have you ever heard someone share that they are emotionally tired?

_____

_____

4. What effect do you think bad or good communication can have on a person's emotions?

_____

_____

_____

_____

FINANCES, IS IT RELEVANT TO OUR HEALTH?

One's finances help to shape how we live. If we lack, then survival is low and zero-rated. If we have abundance, then great things can be achieved. If we are to be fair to ourselves and others, we were never placed on earth to be in want. Should we consistently have needs, there is no way we can help ourselves, our families, and those we serve or meet.

Arguably, does having money alone make us healthy? We mentioned emotions, values, spirituality, and other life issues above. Financially, a person can incorporate these practices to create wealth and health. For example, a person's emotional intelligence is the number one soft skill for any job or career. If a worker has difficulty relating to his colleagues, this may result in delayed promotions or being chosen less for special assignments.

Man's achievement allows him to move forward positively. Success breathes success.

The Bible says when a person's mind is renewed daily, it enables better thought processes and results.

Other areas that promote financial and healthy gains are further studies and serving others.

As we serve, we are empowered to learn from these experiences and to impart knowledge to our communities.

In service, we can develop in areas we may not have anticipated. Consequently, others need us, and we need them.

Networking or fellowshipping is vital to survival. Again, no man is an island. We depend on the people in the bank, the schools, the city offices, and other service areas to grow and improve the unexpected.

We develop our minds to make the right choices to earn. Likewise, we must seek ways to help others.

Suze Orman has produced videos and books on how to succeed financially. Some of the videos highlight how to reduce student and personal loans. Suze advised her audience to pay off their student loans before venturing into other expenses or loan types. Practicing paying off loans can inculcate responsible behavioral patterns and a healthier mindset.

"Robbing Peter to pay Paul" should not be a lifestyle we aim to maintain. Also, with the emergence of digital applications without credit checks, purchasing items and paying them back later should only be for emergencies. While we can agree that applications such as Affirm, AfterPay, and myriad other popular American applications and ClearPay (United Kingdom) can assist consumers in receiving products before they have the full purchase price; it should never be a regular way of spending.

Hence, we must be prudent in the way we spend. The concept is to manage one's finances to induce peace and well-being. We should never overextend ourselves. The adage, "live within your means" is still relevant today. Culture remains beautiful as we realize we have similar issues yet are managed differently.

SELF REFLECTION QUESTIONS

1. What does managing your finances or money mean to you?

   _____

   _____

   _____

   _____

   _____

2. Have you seen a documentary or watched an online story about healthy finance?

   _____

   _____

   _____

3. Please share more about the good financial information you have gained.

_____

_____

_____

_____

4. Do you visualize being financially stable in five or ten years?

_____

7

WHAT DOES HISTORY AND BIBLIOLOGY HAVE TO DO WITH US NOW?

Honestly, culture has been considered beautiful from the beginning of time. From a Biblical perspective, if the Book of Acts - Chapter 2:46-47 were to be used as a source, we can see that the Apostles, (all Galileans) gathered and prayed in different languages (tongues). The people of diverse cultures heard what the apostles said and were able to understand as their different languages were spoken.

Biblical history continues to depict that men seek favor from each other. A man fights for authority. Man misunderstands the other. The Book of Hebrews 11 verse 3 states, "The world was shaped by the word of God". Despite this knowledge, conflicts exist. Another scripture says in the Book of Genesis 1, In the beginning, God created the heaven and the earth…and verses 5 and 6, continue to say, "And God called the light Day, and the darkness he called Night and the evening, and the morning were the first of the day. And God said, let there be a firmament in the waters…" (Genesis 1: 1, 5, and 6)

History shows that most families enjoy each other over meals. It is time to gather, savor the meals, and learn more about each other. Some gather to show respect for the elderly.

Each family had different ways of gathering. Culturally, Jamaican families are known to sit down to a meal, especially on Sundays. They cook large dishes with two to four types of meat as part of the main course. Candidly, in watching the weekly law enforcement TV series: "Blue Blood", what rings admirable is that the family makes it quite important to gather every Sunday, pray, and eat a meal.

Even though history writes about the current behavior and thought process of its people, it started from Earth's inception. Adam and Eve's behavior in the Garden of Eden expresses why there is pain, cheating, and misunderstanding, and why Earth needs order.

It also speaks to the breaking away of families resulting in vast misunderstandings and prejudice.

As we look down through time, the emergence of the abolition of slavery, women in the workplace, disabilities laws, the right to vote, and many civil rights laws, for example, have paved the way to better societies. However, some cultures or nations struggle with some thinking or practices. This is mainly because of a lack of resources.

America has shown itself as Number One for centuries as it has supported and written laws to protect its people and continues to do so. Each nation has the potential to empower its people to believe in what they have. Using one's resources can strengthen a nation and bring confidence.

Alternatively, countries can negotiate or trade resources beneficially if they partner. As we saw earlier, we may have various countries meeting under different umbrellas such as WHO (World Health Organization) to bargain or negotiate resources for their people's enhancement or a better way of life.

A country with stronger health resources can negotiate during these meetings to supply the weaker nations.

Thus, the negotiation resolves to supply a country constantly until they have developed their resources. Or the arrangements can be for supplies to be readily dispatched for disasters such as hurricanes. We see this vividly displayed whenever one country has a state of emergency, such as after a storm passes.

Likewise, international trade occurs to resolve these issues. Everyone benefits. It is synonymous with a business economy of scale, where there is growth, the benefits can spread.

Briefly viewing trade policies, merchandise philosophy started in the 16th and 17th centuries, mainly in European nations where gold was a prime merchandise. Though there were trade laws, countries benefited from each other, and as the people and times evolved, so did the laws over time. Hence, the World Bank can be a prime example of nations collaborating around the cost of their trade analysis.

Also, as the Bible states, 'iron sharpened iron". No one can survive on their own. No country or community can maintain itself alone. Proverbs 27:17 NIV: "As iron sharpens iron, so one person sharpens another".

Biblically, we see stories portraying this. In Matthew 25:14-25:30, a master gave away some talents to his servants before he went on his business trip. One got five, the second two, and the third received one talent.

The servant with the five talents invested or traded them and earned five more. The second traded his two talents and earned twice the amount. The last did not invest but buried the one he was given.

Upon the master's return, the first and second reported their successes, while the last servant told him he buried it as he was afraid. Another scripture states, "For everyone to whom much is given, much is required (expected)". (Luke 12:48) Therefore, since the last servant did nothing with his talent, he was not promoted like the two other servants who made gains for their master. Consequently, his one talent was taken away from him and given to the first servant, who got both a promotion and a bonus.

Give and you will receive. Your gift will return to you in full... (Luke 6:38 NLT)

> Give, and it will be given to you. A good measure, pressed down, shaken together, and running over, will be poured into your lap. For with the measure you use, it will be measured to you".
>
> Luke 6:38 (NIV)

As we develop, respecting each other's strength(s) determines positive outcomes. In Ephesians 4:11-13, "Now these are the gifts Christ gave to the church: the apostles, the prophets, the evangelists, and the pastors and teachers. Their responsibility is to equip God's people to do his work and build up the church, the body of Christ. This will continue until we all unite in our faith and knowledge of God's Son that we will be mature in the Lord, measuring up to the complete standard of Christ".

If each leader respects his colleague's role in developing his sheep (the congregants), much more can be achieved. In addition, each leader has more time to focus and do an excellent job. For example, if the teacher does a great job teaching his students, he strengthens the office of a pastor who frequently is the leader of that structure.

Similarly, organizations have always had each department with its area of specialization. Each department exists to strengthen the other, thus benefiting the whole company's vision and mission. For example, the accounting department's primary goal is the organization's finances; however, to keep a robust company vision alive, it interrelates with the manufacturing department and guides it on managing its funds, for example, the cost of the material needed.

Historically, we have had several types of integration in the business departmental efficiency, such as emailing a chart or report. However, with the emergence of electronic or technological interlocking, each department's systems were developed to mitigate confusion or risk. One such program is Microsoft Office. Microsoft Office allows Teams to integrate electronically and collaborate with Outlook and SharePoint. Groups are formed within these systems. Some areas get shared with the relevant teams and departments. Importantly, each department is working towards a common cause or goal. SharePoint allows departments to assist each other in real-time, avoid confusion, and correct errors ahead of time.

Consequently, members are more prepared for meetings. Understanding unfamiliar terms within their diverse local and global settings ahead of time.

As with organizations, so it is with families. A family of seven children and the same parents may think differently, though they display some common traits. As a result, each child chooses a different profession; his goal is usually to ensure his family is taken care of.

These examples can be traced as far back as history or Biblical times.

One more cultural perspective tying into historical and biblical data is the role of immigrants. This may be a taboo subject; however, it is simple. Let us look at the story with Joseph. Though his brothers sold him into Egypt, he mightily served his boss (Potiphar) and stayed in his favor until calamity came and he was unfairly imprisoned. Because he did well among the prisoners, he was well-liked, which served as a reference to him being appointed into the boss' office again and no sooner received a promotion to becoming the overseer or President/Prime Minister over Egypt. As we can see in this concise synopsis, Joseph was an immigrant sold as a slave out of Israel who gained favor in Egypt because he served well.

While that was in the 1900 BC, developing nations continued to have biases or prejudices through language, race, ethnicity, gender, sexuality, religion, and so on. As prejudice remains, nations constantly misunderstand each other. Unfair practices occur within homes, communities, organizations, churches, countries, and the House of Representatives. We could discuss these at length; however, I will leave this for other volumes of this book with in-depth studies.

I will not fail to mention that as countries develop, the exodus continues. We see this in Joseph's era. The Book of Genesis speaks to the bondage of the people while the Exodus speaks to the redemption of its people. Many dynamic events occurred during the period from Genesis to Exodus. Trading and the thought process of its people were highly misconstrued, causing rumors of war. In the Book of Exodus, Moses was the one God appointed to lead his people to freedom, exemplifying the population being redeemed.

Redemption can be inferred here as offering a better way of life.

We have developed and changed, yet we are the same. That is, we remain fighting for freedom: freedom to understand others, to choose land, to decide where we live, and other similar concerns. Over the years, we have seen many exoduses. A group of Japanese left their country for the United States seeking peace and prosperity for their families, especially their children. As a result, they became one of the major populations in Hawaii.

Also, in the early 20th Century, naval vessels were enlisted to transport bananas from tropical countries to the United States and Europe. Over time, these sea vessels were called, "banana boats". They not only carried bananas but also passengers from other countries deemed oppressed. As people were looking for a better way of life, that method of transportation was the resolution.

Of course, we saw diseases and many other concerning factors among the passengers due to being cramped in the vessels or stemming from the depression they experienced before traveling. Today, we see similar "border crossings" still being experienced, which has caused many political battles among nations.

However, people who migrate to a nation have their share of respect or none. This behavior stemmed from the bad taste of history. Consequently, immigrants who, for example, are legal will find themselves less understood. Again, we can discuss this in the next volume of this book.

As developed people, have we ever wondered why a group of persons from another nation chose to live in their host country or what benefit the immigrant provides to the community? Simply put, each person has a lot to offer. An immigrant may bring skills that a country or organization needs to accomplish a task. This mindset can lead to the immigrant and his Host Country reaping benefits and strengthening a nation.

For example, Jill may bring skills in her native language or the customs of her birth country. As she gains employment, her first language can benefit her company, where she can effectively communicate with customers, clients, and traders. During project meetings, she can be the Subject Matter Expert; her knowledge of the culture, business ethics, or trade can assist in decision-making. Thus, as with the man with the five talents, she can obtain much more for her cooperation. Additionally, the company will have gains like the boss in the story.

As we revise the inception of time, conflicts were not resolved or understood, so man remains in stagnant mindsets, or the cycle continues. If we do not realize that we all make up the whole, then a better standard of living or way of life cannot be effectively achieved.

WE. CANNOT. IGNORE. THE. STRENGTHS. OF. OTHERS.

WE. MUST. ACKNOWLEDGE. EACH. OTHERS. STRENGTH. FOR. BETTER. COMMUNITIES.

SELF REFLECTION QUESTIONS

1. Do you see how history or Bibliology is connected to modern or current times?

   _____

2. Are there any historical or Biblical references that quickly come to mind after reading this chapter?

   _____

   _____

   _____

3. Are you interested in exploring historical or Biblical facts or stories?

   _____

4. Can you discuss what you learned with your family, classmates, friends, and co-workers or colleagues?

   _____

   _____

   _____

   _____

EATING: I LIKE THAT; NO! NO, I LOVE THAT

As we saw in previous chapters, most cultures enjoy meals among their families and sometimes friends. How can we differentiate why we eat the foods or have set days to savor a specific meal?

Our culture remains and becomes even more beautiful when we recognize and respect another's way of life and can cohabit. Isn't it great to see someone else eat meat while another may not practice this? For example, let us look at the community that may eat frog legs. Since Jane never socialized to eat those tender meats, it does not mean that it is not good for the other person who does.

Most Asians, some Spanish countries or islands, the United States of America, and France serve frog legs as delicacies. Since they provide Vitamin A, protein, Omega-3, and potassium, these nations must naturally have seen their value; consequently, the meal becomes more enjoyable. On the other hand, a culture not familiar with this delicacy may not consider its value.

Likewise, the well-known African and American leafy green collard greens may not be favored by other nations since they are unfamiliar with their nutrients. To ensure and appreciate different cultures, this example can be compared to the Jamaican callaloo - also a leafy green vegetable. It can provide similar nourishment, yet the texture and preparation of each differ. The same goes for the spinach. While spinach is a leafy green vegetable, it can be prepared in many ways and dishes. Collard greens and callaloo can be creatively prepared in several dishes. The only differences found would be preparation time and availability of resources.

Collards and spinach are in almost every grocery store in the United States; however, callaloo is mainly in Caribbean or International stores. It is an expensive commodity due to import and export tariffs or mark-ups.

Interestingly, Naturalized US Citizens of Jamaican heritage are famous for growing the callaloo in their backyards. Tip: if you need to validate a Jamaican's lineage, look for callaloo sprouts thriving in his backyard garden. Of course, while it is widely grown in Jamaica, the local Jamaican grocery stores and markets carry it too.

Some cultures are adaptable to other cultural foods, others are not. Chinese and Italian dishes are well-liked across nations. Some love a plate of Italian savories and practice cooking the meals at home. In the United States, some States are known for certain savory dishes. Texas is known for its iconic chicken fried steak, chili, and pecan pie. North Carolina for its barbecue and southern-style cooking.

Over the centuries, we have realized that people from different cultures gather and enjoy each other's food or menu. Workplaces and colleges have cultural days. Internet space has opened doors to influencers who anxiously introduce their native meals thus inducing appreciation and intrigue.

I remember my stay at the Hilton Hotel in Sandton, Johannesburg, South Africa in 2022. Oxtail was on the menu for dinner one evening. I tried it. Although it was not cooked the Jamaican way, it was just as savory and spicy - the meat fell off the bone. It was mighty delicious.

On the other hand, I have visited other countries that serve food I am not accustomed to consuming. However, combatting this, I travel with snacks I like and call ahead to determine which foods the hotel may have to assist with my planning. Sometimes, I feel audacious and look forward to trying the different meals.

Appreciation for one another is critical to living amicably in our environments or communities. Remove the racial jargon, old mindset, or stagnant way of life or thought process for a little while, and we will see that we are already enjoying each other.

Challenge ourselves to intentionally meet another person who is not from a similar background and see how we can learn. Keep an open mindset.

SELF REFLECTION QUESTIONS

1. Are there foods from any other cultures you would like to taste?

_____

2. Were any unfamiliar foods mentioned in the chapter that you would like to explore?

_____

_____

3. How do you feel about joining a party, a class function, or a get-together to explore different ethnic dishes?

_____

_____

4. Are you ready to travel to another country to experience their ethnic meals?

_____

_____

5. Would you like to share your ethnic meals with colleagues, friends, or classmates?

_____

_____

LANGUAGE / COMMUNICATION – DO WE UNDERSTAND EACH OTHER?

The bold radiance of our different languages provides unique combinations for all people. Everyone communicates with each other, though our languages may differ. Each language has its consonance. Some tongues are used differently to provide the sounds. Some cultures speak the same language but use another word to describe a thing. Can't you hear the beauty coming out right now?

Conversely, when I speak with an Australian, though the English Language is used, the sound with word pronunciations rings melodious in my ear. On the other hand, another person may find it too much, and the communication or response to that person results in the wrong tone.

During communication, tone is always important in conveying a message. Is my tone respectful or aggressive, for example? While we are on the matter of language, respect is vital. Some cultures or countries commonly use a formal tone to communicate while others use a more relaxed style.

We have varying languages across cultures. Whether the language is English, Spanish, French, or Mandarin, it is important to discover a common ground to communicate. For example, when International Conferences such as Caricom Heads of Government, G15 (Group of 17 Developing Countries), and World Health Organization (WHO) meet, participants must understand that communicating is crucial. Whether an interpreter is available for the participants, understanding a simple greeting may be the best way to start conversations.

Great international conference organizers train their workers in the customs or practices of participating countries for better communication and success.

As previously mentioned, most countries recognize a handshake as a greeting; however, others practice other ways of greeting. In some countries, when the greeting is misunderstood, it may portray discourtesy or be offensive.

While some countries in the Caribbean Islands, such as Jamaica, and some in North America commonly recognize the handshake without issues, others do not. A handshake is usually the right hand. Middle Eastern countries use the right hand; the left hand is considered unclean. The Chinese do not acknowledge a strong grip on the hand as favorable. The Germans use a single downward pull to display a firm handshake.

Other forms of greetings involve a kiss on each cheek, an air kiss on the cheek, and greeting your elders before the younger folks, among other styles.

Italy, Spain, Portugal, and most European countries practice the kiss on each cheek.

An air kiss on the right or left cheek is common for South Americans: Colombia, Chile, Argentina, Brazil, and Peru.

Portugal, Spain, and Italy commonly give two air kisses, while Russia and Ukraine give three.

Most Asian cultures greet the elder first as a sign of respect and to gain favor.

Some cultures such as the Caribbeans and Europeans spell words differently, though they mean the same thing. The United States of America (USA) spells 'favor' without the letter 'u'. Interestingly, the Caribbeans and Europeans spell it with the 'u': "favour".

Other similar differences are: -

USA English	Caribbean/ European English	Explanations
Flavor	Flavour	
Check	Cheque	Method of payment
Behavior	Behaviour	
Color	Colour	
Jewelry	Jewellery	
Gray	Grey	Color
Meter	Metre	Measurement

It is beautiful to view the differences, and these are just a few. It is all English Language but has its differences.

Likewise, most Spanish-speaking nations differ in their words and dialects.

Studies show that most immigrants continue to speak and spell their language from their Mother Tongue. Some find it difficult to adjust. I interviewed some American immigrants. Though they learned most of the differences, at times, there is a need to refer to research to be reminded of their current country's ways. For example, most American organizations do not practice using 'kindly' in oral or written communication. However, more formal cultures such as the Caribbeans, Africans, and Europeans continue to use it. A word of caution, practice using the country's ways of life, as it facilitates better communication and understanding among communities. This befits a common adage: When in Rome, do as the Romans do.

On the contrary, in cultures that do not use a word, people can have a healthy understanding that another subset of their population still does use their learned language. Knowing this can develop healthier friendships and work allies.

Another noticeable communication practice is writing a letter or an email. Formal settings still use "Dear" as the salutation. However, correspondents in the USA mainly use "Hi." Occasionally, "dear" may be found in company correspondence but is not practiced, as the preferred way is saying "hi" instead. The significance is that the USA tends to use a more relaxed culture.

Communication is vital regardless of language or cultural practices. Studies share that we communicate more through body language than orally. Others say it is arguable, as the conclusion originated from Albert Mehrabian's research with a sample of one hundred-plus students and not a wide population. Be that as it may, communication lends to watching and listening for cues that can stimulate healthier feedback and understanding.

Another study by two psychologists. In 1955, Joseph Luft and Harrington Ingham developed the Johari Window. According to Luft and

Ingham, this psychological model can assist in understanding ourselves and others. It is also considered a model to develop interpersonal skills for personal or business purposes.

The Johari Window is used by businesses in team-building sessions. However, I posit that it can also be used to help us understand and communicate better with each other.

JOHARI WINDOW

1. *OPEN*	2. *BLIND*
Known to Self and Others	Not known to self but known to others
3. *HIDDEN*	4. *UNKNOWN*
Known to self but not to others	Not known to self or others

If the quadrant is studied successfully, users can be better equipped to communicate and understand each other.

Looking at Window 1 – it declares that this is the obvious. For example, if I am wearing a green dress and others can see it as the same color, then it is obvious.

Window 2 – I may not know it, but others do. It is often called a blind spot. Scientifically or in the field of vision, a blind spot is what we cannot see. The retina, for example, cannot see an area due to lack of light; it is just dark. It is usually recommended to see a doctor. For example, drivers can be hindered from seeing an object causing an accident. However, figuratively speaking, as it is for the eye's retina failure, similarly, someone may fail to accept or understand a matter. Likewise, a person can choose to be biased or ignorant resulting in improper or inaccurate decisions. Lastly, a person can decide not to judge or discriminate, as it does not matter about another's origin, as this person is seen as a human being.

Window 3 – it is known to me and not others. The subject may say I am deciding to keep this secret to stay safe. Therefore, part of the study calls it a façade. For example, Sue went to a dinner party held by her company. The party attendees were mainly elites. So as not to appear out of place, she got the most expensive dress, studied the people's names and involvement, and fitted in nicely with them. She was able to converse with others effectively.

Window 4 – I and others do not know the information – this window can seem dangerous; however, an interpretation of this is that of the unknown. The unknown can be viewed as spiritual and only be made known to a person if he spends time with the Supreme: God. The Bible says God is all-knowing. If I need to understand a hidden truth about myself, spending time with God can unfold that truth.

Ultimately, interpersonal skills can be developed. As we look at each Window, improving oneself can take time. Consequently, understanding and developing relationships with these factors in mind can aid in better communicating with others.

Interpersonal skills do not become valuable unless we communicate. I have a favorite phrase, "Know Thyself". As we develop in this changing world, it is important to use the resources available to make better communicators, friends, and workers. It may sound cliché to say, "Each one needs one". It is true; the language of the other, whether figurative, or literal, brings beautiful sounds for nations to become better with each other, families, peers, and colleagues.

****

> While Edmora's article outlined the American and British word Differences, I want to capture some variances here.

AMERICAN	BRITISH	DIFFERENCES
Criticize	Criticise	Ending with ze or se
Realize	Realise	
Emphasize	Emphasise	Studies show preference is given to the word Emphasize in both culture/nation
Center	centre	Organization or building
Program	Programme	
Aluminum	Aluminium	Metal
Airplane	Aeroplane	Air vehicle
License	Licence	Driving Permit
Mom	Mum	Mother
Deposit	lodge	Place money in bank
Check	Cheque	Method of payment

Edmora highlighted a few more vocabulary differences between the British and American systems or cultures.

BRITISH	AMERICAN	EXPLAINED
Rubbish	Trash	
Bonnet	Hood	Front of the car
Dust bin	Garbage can	
Postcode	Zip Code	
Sweets	Candy	
Lift	Elevator	
Tap	Faucet	
Rubber	Eraser	

These are fun words to view and please visit Edmora's page to learn other similar ones.

[British English Vs. American English: Key Differences and Comparison - Edmora](#)

SELF REFLECTIVE QUESTIONS

1. Have you experienced being unsure how to greet or compliment someone?
   _____

2. Have you ever experienced any forms of different communication or greeting?
   _____

3. Have you tried practicing another language or cultural behavior?
   _____

NAME WORDS LEARNED AND WHAT YOU GAINED FROM THIS CHAPTER

WHICH WORDS OR CULTURAL EXPRESSIONS WOULD YOU LIKE TO EXPLORE?

PERSONAL NOTES TO SELF

PERSONAL NOTES TO SELF

NOTES OF MY GOALS TO EXPLORE MY KNOWLEDGE & SKILL SET

FRIENDS AND FAMILY TO INCLUDE IN MY NETWORK OF EXPLORATIONS

GLOSSARY

A _____

ABRAHAM

The first name of a male. In this context of the book, Abraham Maslow was an American psychologist.

ACTS

The fifth book in the New Testament of the Bible

ACTUALIZATION

A person's realization that something is achievable and does happen.

AFFIRM

An online, digital application used to shop online or in-store. Affirm allows the shopper to repay the amount in a flexible monthly repayment plan.

AFTERPAY

A digital application is used to shop online or in-store. Afterpay allows the shopper to repay the amount in a flexible monthly repayment plan.

ALPH

A person's (usually a male) first name. In this case, the male was Pastor Alph Lukau.

ANGLICAN

The Anglican Church, also known as Episcopalian in the US uses a Christian practice (belief that Jesus Christ is Lord and Savior) to conduct their daily lives and services. The Anglican church was first established in Britain.

APPEAL

A legal proceeding where a case is presented before a higher court for review or rehearing of a lower court's proceeding.

ASIAN

An individual from the Asian Continent (China, Japan, India, or countries in that continent).

ASPERGER

Asperger's Syndrome = part of the autism spectrum disorder (ASD). A person with the syndrome may have difficulty communicating with others, use repetitive actions, or follow strict routines compulsively.

AUTISM

A condition in an individual's brain development that may impact their ability to communicate effectively.

B

BANKRUPTCY

A state of financial insolvency or loss in which a person or business can use a legal process to manage indebtedness and start over.

BIBLIOLOGY

The doctrine of the Bible – a belief that God has revealed Himself in several ways such as through history, creation, miracles, and visions given directly to prophets.

C

CALALOO

A green leafy vegetable eaten in the Caribbean namely from the island of Jamaica.

CAPITALIST

A person who runs a business to make a profit for himself. Also, a person who supports capitalism. Capitalism is an economic and political system where private owners control their properties, businesses, and industries instead of the state, to make a profit.

CARIBBEAN

Countries such as Cuba, Hispaniola, Jamaica, and Puerto Rico, are islands surrounded by the Caribbean Sea. The islands are Northeast of North America, East of Central America, and Northwest of South

America, and are known for their captivating blue water beaches, and individual unique cultures.

CATHOLIC

A Christian denomination from the Roman Catholic Church led by a succession of Popes.

CLEARPAYS

See Afterpay – Clearpay is the United Kingdom's online digital application like the United States' Afterpay for purchases.

COLLARD

A green leafy vegetable from the cabbage, mustard, or kale family; also called collard greens.

COMMUNIST

A person who believes in a social and political ideology that attempts to develop a classless society in which all property and wealth are publicly owned, instead of owned by individuals. This is the opposite of capitalism.

CULTURE

The way of life of people who share the same values, practices, and beliefs.

D_____

DEMOCRATIC

A society where the people rule. The people vote for a leader. A democratic process is where the people vote for what is best for a group in society.

E_____

EMOTIONS

Emotions are strong or convincing feelings such as love. Strong feelings can also be anger or similar emotions.

ETHNICITY

A group or subgroup sharing a common descent or cultural background.

EUROPEAN

Inhabitants of Europe. Europeans are from Great Britain, Italy, France, Spain, Greece, or any other European country.

EXODUS

The second Book in the Old Testament of the Bible. It can also mean mass departure of a people from one place to another as described in the book of Exodus.

F_____

FURLOUGH

It is a temporary type of redundancy. A company lays off its employees temporarily as there is no work to disperse. Staff can be called back to work when assignments are available.

FREEMASONS

A male fraternal or secret society where members help each other and use secret signs to communicate.

G_____

GALILEANS

A native of Galilee. Galilee is in northern Israel and Southern Lebanon.

GENESIS

The first Book of the Bible.

GLOBALLY

A concept of including all parts of a situation or involving the world.

H_____

HAWAIIAN

Residents of the state of Hawaii. Hawaiians are mainly of Polynesian descent.

HIERARCHY

A grading system where persons or things are ranked above the other as in Maslow's Hierarchy.

I_____

IMMIGRANTS

A population who left their birthplace to live in a foreign country.

J_____

JAMAICAN

Natives of the Caribbean Island of Jamaica.

JAPANESE

The language belongs to the natives of Japan.

JEWS

A population who practices Judaism. They trace their origin back to the ancient Hebrew nation of Israel to Abraham.

L_____

LAISSEZ-FAIRE

A system that lets people in the marketplace make decisions regarding goods and prices without any interference. It is also an economic system that refuses Government interference in companies' business affairs.

M_____

MANDARIN

A standard Chinese language that is spoken mainly in the cities of Beijing, Shanghai, and parts of Taiwan.

MITIGATE

To lessen the severity or harshness of a situation.

MONARCHIST

A monarchist or a royalist is an individual who independently supports the government of Kings and Queens.

MUSLIM

A population following the religion of Islam. A religion indicating there is only one God which is a belief belonging to the Abrahamic tradition. Their religious text is the Quran.

N_____

NAVAL

It is related to the navy, military ships, or warships.

O_____

OUTLOOK

Outlook is a program or email service from the Microsoft family.

P_____

POLITICAL

A system that allows how a country is run.

Q_____

QUADRANT

A quadrant is each of a four-part object such as a plane, building, or circle.

R_____

RELIGION

A belief that there is a superpower above a natural one.

RETINA

It is a cell at the back of the eyeball

S_____

SAUDI ARABIA

Saudi Arabia is a lightly populated country. It is officially called the Kingdom of Saudi Arabia and ruled and founded by the Saud family. It is in West Asia in the center of the Middle East.

SHAREPOINT

SharePoint is a part of the Microsoft Office family. This tool can be used to share information among groups. Most organizations use it to keep specific groups informed. It is also widely used among project managers to organize, store, and access information from any device when needed.

SOCIALIST

A person who practices socialism. Socialism is a political system that advocates for the common man's ownership of the public system or management of property or resources.

SPIRITUALITY

Spirituality is where an individual seeks to be connected to something higher than himself, looking for purpose, meaning, and peace. The common practice when doing so is through prayer and meditation.

The biblical meaning of spirituality is evidenced through the fruit of the Spirit (Galatians 5:22-23) and guided by the Holy Spirit of God. Spiritual maturity and holiness are generated from the Spirit of God.

SQUAREUP

It is a payment method used by individuals and businesses. It pays for purchases and purchasers receive a repayment plan.

T_____

TABOO

A consensus to do or talk about something publicly as it is not acceptable in a religious or social setting.

TRADE

The exchange of one item for another. In commerce, it is an exchange of goods and services among countries, businesses, and individuals.

V_____

VALUES

Values are beliefs that guide us to make beneficial decisions.

VENEZUELA

Venezuela is a South American country.

VISA

A document or authorized stamp in a traveler's passport permitting them to travel legally to a country.

VOODOO

Voodoo is a religious form of African worship with magic. It is typically used in Haiti and the Southern USA with magic, traditional medicine, and ancestral practices.

W_____

WITCHCRAFT

Witchcraft is a term usually applied to cause hurt to others using supernatural or occult powers, or magic.

WORLD HEALTH ORGANIZATION (WHO)

WHO is a specialized agency founded in 1948 to focus on international public health. Its main base is in Geneva, Switzerland.

Z_____

ZUCCHETTO

It is the Catholic leader's headgear.

BIBLIOGRAPHY

1. Cline, Austin, (2019). What's the Difference Between Religion versus Spirituality?

2. Cooper, W. E. (1992). William James's theory of the self. The Monist, 75 (4), 504-520.

3. Covey, Stephen R. (2006). Habit 5 -- Seek First to Understand, Then to Be Understood: The Habit of Mutual Understanding

4. Davies, Suzy, (2017). Johari's Window

5. Hwang, Hyisung C., and Matsumoto, David (September 2016). The Expression of Emotion

6. - Philosophical, Psychological, and Legal Perspectives - Edited by Catharine Abell and Joel Smith

7. The Holy Bible – AMP; NIV, English Version

8. Maslow, Abraham H. (2013). A Theory of Human Motivation, revised edition

9. Orman, Suze, (2014). DO'S AND DONT'S OF MONEY Easy Solutions for Everyday Problems

10. Thorndike, Jonathan L. (2015). Library of Congress. Japanese | Immigration and Relocation in U.S. History | Classroom Materials at the Library of Congress | Library of Congress

11. Ciolli, Chris, (May 18, 2023). Here's How People Greet Each Other Around the World.

12. 10 Different Greetings from Around the World - AFAR

13. Picchi, Aimee (April 27, 2020). MoneyWatch

14. Furloughed due to the coronavirus? Here's what you need to know

15. https://www.cbsnews.com/news/furlough-versus-layoff-unemployment-aid-coronavirus/

16. Rivera, Daniel, (December 13, 2024). British English Vs. American English: Key Differences and Comparison – Edmora - https://edmora.org/british-english-vs-american-english-key-differences-and-comparison/

12

ABOUT THE AUTHOR

Audith Johnson, fondly called Audie J., is known for serving her community and leading projects at work, home, and church.

In addition to her projects, she successfully wrote and produced three plays. These plays received high acclaim and were well attended. She believes in the art of her work. Audith's work aims to didactically impart a better way of life via biblical and environmental lenses.

She is from Kingston, Jamaica, and has served in the Government for 15 years. She spent four years in the Quasi-Government (Coffee Industry Board), and 11 years in the classroom teaching Language Arts and Reading.

Her years in the private sector total 12 years, with a specialization in marketing and hospitality.

She loves family, and has one child, Renee', and she loves to watch her achieve her goals.

www.ingramcontent.com/pod-product-compliance
Lightning Source LLC
Chambersburg PA
CBHW070100100426
42743CB00012B/2607